Written by Jenni Avery
Copyright © 2023 All rights reserved.
Published by Wild Lark Books

Photography by Carleigh Madeleine Photography
Cover Design by Brianne van Reenen

Wild Lark Books
513 Broadway Street
Lubbock, Texas 79401
wildlarkbooks.com

#supportartreadbooks

No part of this publication may be reproduced, stored electronically. or transmitted in any form without written permission of the publisher or author.

To request permission, please use the following contact information:
Wild Lark Books - info@wildlarkbooks.com

Family & Relationships | Biography
ISBN 9781957864693
eBook ISBN 9781957865709

All names used with permission.

Bulk and wholesale orders can be made directly through the publisher through the information provided above.

THE DUMB BLONDE'S GUIDE TO DIVORCE

Note from the Publisher

WILD LARK BOOKS

Wild Lark Books is an independent publisher that supports authors as artists. As with all works of art, reviews help build readerships and increase the impact of this book.

If Jenni's story has impacted you as a reader, please help support her artistry by leaving reviews online, sharing about it on social media using #dumbblondesguidetodivorce, or speaking about it to all your friends and family.

Your support would mean the worlds to us.

Thank you!

Wild Lark Books
Support Art. Read Books.

The Dumb Blonde's Guide to Divorce

JENNI AVERY

WILD LARK BOOKS

To all of the women who know something isn't right.
Listen to yourself.

Contents

Dedication		vii
1	The Dumb Blonde	1
2	Let Him Underestimate You	5
3	Document Everything	7
4	Keep Your House Clean	11
5	Find a Support Group	14
6	Hire an Attorney Who Gives a Crap	17
7	Get Your Divorce "Degree"	24
8	Look Through Every Piece of Discovery Yourself	27
9	Read EVERYTHING - And Ask Questions	30
10	Don't Forget Your WHY	32
11	Know When to Walk Away - Know When to RUN	36
12	Take Care of Yourself	38
13	Every Little Bit Helps	41
14	Dumb Blonde?	44
Acknowledgements		49
About The Author		53

Chapter 1

The Dumb Blonde

I know I'm not dumb. Heck, I'm not actually a real blonde anymore either. Shhhh. Don't tell anyone. LOL

But I chose this title because I believed I was dumb. If I stopped and thought about it, I knew I wasn't dumb. I know I am a smart, talented, creative woman. Well, I know that now anyway.

This book is for anyone who was convinced she was stupid.

Were you told he would take care of the finances because he wanted to make sure they actually got paid? Subtle.

Did he tell you he wouldn't share a checking account with anyone ever again because his first wife bounced checks all of the time?

Or maybe he wasn't controlling and manipulative. Maybe he was being completely true, honest, and without an agenda, but it kept you in the dark about your finances just the same.

Now you're getting divorced. Well, this guide is for you.

I was conditioned for years to believe I was nothing without my spouse. He told me I couldn't survive without him. He told me our business's "doors will be closed within one year of the divorce." He said, with his cocky, head tilt, "Jenni, you know you don't understand business." He said many other things that conditioned me to doubt myself. I was manipulated for 20 years to believe the crap he wanted me to believe. So, of course, it was hard to believe in myself and it was easy to second guess my talents, abilities and well, myself. I bought into this gaslighting, and it took something really bad to open my eyes so I would stand up for myself and our son and leave that abusive relationship.

As you read this, you might wonder why I don't go into much detail about what caused my marriage to fall apart. I am leaving these things out to protect our children. And, you will notice, I don't use my ex's name a single time. This book isn't about bashing him. It is about my journey and how I can, hopefully, help you through yours, but I want you to know that my marriage and divorce almost broke me. To put it in perspective, my daddy died tragically when I was 16 years old. I was with my ex for 23 years. I don't know which loss was more devastating. I do know that both men and both losses completely changed me and my life. Through my journey I have learned that, sometimes, the devastation of loss and love can lead to something beautiful; something I never knew I had. The devastation of my old life forced me to use all of my strength and fortitude to create a better, healthier version of myself. So, I can relate to your overwhelming pain, loss, and fear.

When I started the divorce process, my self-esteem was in the toilet. I spent my life searching for a hero. When I met my ex, I believed he was that hero, my Prince Charming. I truly believed he was the best thing that had ever happened to me. He gave me a family, a home. He isn't an entirely bad person. He can't be. The kids are half him so he can't be all bad. But he definitely wasn't a hero.

Now don't get me wrong, I'm not perfect either. I'm not trying to say that I am all that is perfect and light and that I have a halo around my head. I am an imperfect person who does the best I can. I try to live my life by a code. I believe if we would all just do what is right, the world would be a pretty great place. I try to live by the Golden Rule, "Do unto others as you would have done unto you." And, I try to have compassion and grace for my fellow man because I would like to receive compassion and grace. I have made my own fair share of mistakes and I believe that people who live in glass houses should not throw stones. I also believe in Karma.

I wrote this book to help others who are in situations like mine. I hope to help you feel less alone. I hope this book helps you build your own self-confidence and self-esteem. I want you to know you ARE strong enough. You ARE capable of taking care of yourself and fighting for what is fair and right. You now have a friend to lean on in all the hard moments. And you are NOT a dumb blonde (or brunette or redhead). You are a Blondie. Simply stated, YOU ARE ENOUGH!

I told you about that hero I was looking for. Well, she was staring at me in the mirror every day. I just had to open my eyes and see her. I hope you find your hero in the mirror too.

Now for the Disclaimer:

I am by no means a legal expert. The purpose of this book is to tell you what I did that helped me and how I did it. I also tell you what I did that I wish I had not done, and I tell you what I didn't know that I wish I did so I could have done some things differently.

Most of us have never been divorced and we never planned on getting divorced. I didn't. I believed in the fairy tale. That's what I thought I was getting. I wasn't prepared to get divorced. Hopefully, my book will help prepare you for something you couldn't imagine.

I am not saying that if you follow the ideas in this book, you will "win". First of all, I'm pretty sure there are no winners in divorce, just different levels of casualty. And secondly, your divorce is probably very different from mine. Everyone has different circumstances. I just hope to help you feel less powerless. Even though I am the one who "wanted the divorce", so to speak, I still loved my husband. I didn't want to get divorced, but I couldn't stay married under those conditions. I was grieving and sometimes my grief was paralyzing. Now, add in the imbalance of power and control within my marriage and it was terrifying. I wrote this book with the hopes it will take some of the terror out of your process.

Chapter 2

Let Him Underestimate You

My ex spent 20 years telling me, with his typical condescending head tilt, that I "don't understand business", telling others I was "just a decoration" and in all sorts of subtle (and not so subtle ways) that I was just a dumb blonde. At some point I started believing him.

Then we separated and I started putting things together in my head. The longer I was out of his direct control, the more I realized I was a lot smarter than I thought. However, I realized HE still thought I was just another dumb blonde. So, I used it to my advantage. I let him think I was stupid. I played HIS game. I just played it better than he did. I asked "stupid" questions that really weren't all that stupid and I documented his answers. After that, I took his responses and compared them to everything else I knew.

Trust your gut!

If something doesn't feel right, it probably isn't.

There were times I had that feeling in my gut and I would try to ignore it, but it wouldn't go away. So, I asked questions. I asked my attorneys and sometimes they didn't think much was going on. But for some reason I kept having these feelings that something wasn't right. I looked into it on my own and guess what??? I found the smoking gun. I found fraud (more than one instance) and conspiracy to commit fraud.

So let him think you are a dumb blonde, or brunette or redhead. Let them think you are just another pretty face with nothing but air between your ears. Use that to your advantage. Let him (and his friends) underestimate you. Just don't underestimate yourself.

You can do this.

Chapter 3

Document Everything

I really wish I had done a better job at this. I keep thinking of the things I could have done that would have helped me; things I could have done to end my suffering sooner. I believe everything happened as it was meant to happen. Perhaps if I had done better, I wouldn't have learned what I learned and I wouldn't have felt the calling to help my fellow Blondies.

Communicate as much as possible via text messaging.

And more importantly, never delete any of them. Back them up and print them out. I used a program called iExplorer but there are others.

Texts turned out to be crucial evidence in my case. During the temporary orders hearing, my ex committed perjury at least four times. Every time I knew he was lying I went to one of my binders and pulled out the texts that proved he was lying. My attorney would keep asking him the same question and he would stick to his story until he was shown the evidence. By the fourth or fifth lie, he glanced at the paper, glared at me, and said he couldn't remember. It is really scary how convincing some liars are. I truly believe, had I not had evidence in black-and-white, the judge would have believed him. He was that good.

Use the search feature in your texts. You can enter a keyword and then scroll through the list to find what you are looking for. For example, if your ex has a drinking problem, search "beer" or "grab a drink" or whatever words he uses. This can help you prove he drinks every day. Or he might have told you something that proves something is community property that he is now claiming is separate. This can be time consuming, but is it really, in the grand scheme of your life?

One more note: Don't forget to look through old phones you might still have. I had to replace my phone about the time I filed for divorce. Luckily, I have saved all of my old phones. I have years and years of texts that prove certain things he claimed are community property were actually gifts. I also have years and years of texts that prove he drank almost daily. All of these things helped my court case.

If he calls you, record the conversation.

I don't think recordings are admissible in some states unless both parties know they are being recorded. Find out the laws that pertain to you. But even if the recordings aren't admissible, they might help you in other ways. I really wish my house had been wired. There are so many more things I could have proven, in court and elsewhere.

However, I still think it is best to communicate through texts. I have a tendency to become emotional, and when we communicated through text, I was able to voice text it (saying it out loud somehow gave me the satisfaction I needed). So, I was able to "say" what I wanted to say. I could then edit the text to make sure I didn't say anything that could come back to hurt me.

I will admit, though, I wasn't always successful at only saying what I should. I was controlled and abused for 20 years. One of my survival methods was to keep my mouth shut. Often, I didn't defend myself in arguments because I was afraid if I engaged, he would get angry and possibly lose his temper. After we separated, I refused to be weak and timid anymore. Sometimes, I let him know exactly what I thought and wouldn't let him walk all over me or have the last word. This was not always the wisest course of action, strategically speaking. However, I do believe it was somewhat healing for me at times. Just be careful.

Social Media

Be careful what you post on social media. I used to be on the board of directors for the College Baseball Foundation. We hosted the College Baseball Hall of Fame inductions and annual college baseball awards show. I loved my ten years on that board and hope to serve again. During my tenure, I met some really great people and heard some really great stories. I will pass one on from when we inducted Nomar Garciaparra. He shared his wisdom with the current college players who were in attendance receiving awards. He told them to never take a picture with alcohol in their hand and to make sure their hands were visible. He was warning them that in this Social Media

Age, a harmless photo can be construed as something inappropriate. It can hurt their image, cost them endorsements, and might ultimately end in a 'he said/she said' legal dispute.

Think of this in your own life. Your ex might save pictures of you with a drink in your hand and try to make it look like to the judge that you party too much. When in fact, you might have only had that one drink the whole night. Also, let's say that over the course of a few months you take photos with several different guy friends. He can twist that to look like you sleep around. I'm not saying he will, but he could.

Conversely, you can look through his social media. You just might find something to help your case. Take screenshots. He might remove you as a friend/follower. He could also delete the post.

And don't forget to go through both of your social media histories. If he is trying to paint you as a bad mom, you can print out examples that prove otherwise. Go through both of your posts. Look for comments he and others made praising your parenting.

Chapter 4

Keep Your House Clean

No, not literally. I mean, you can but anyone who knows me probably wouldn't describe me as housekeeper of the year...or even the week.

The point is to make sure you don't say or do anything that might hurt you.

Let him dig his own grave. Don't dig yours next to him.

In the beginning of the separation, I stumbled a few times and made a couple of bad decisions. I'm not talking about things you go to jail for or cause you to lose custody of your kid. I'm just saying I'm not perfect.

My ex hired a private investigator at some point. I don't know what she found out or even when and how long he employed her. I do know, however, that when we went to our temporary orders hearing, I had evidence of his "dastardly deeds" and he perjured himself a minimum of four times. The worst thing his attorney could say about me??? I bought a dog (which I purposely asked my ex's permission to buy so I couldn't get in trouble for spending that money) and I took our son to watch the Chicago Cubs play the Kansas City Royals (despite his attorney thinking they played the Chiefs-Silly, Stupid man lost his man card with that question). This trip was actually my ex's idea, and he even paid for some of it. He booked our airline tickets, and he purchased some of the tickets to the games for us. Oh, and I could prove all of this with our text message conversations. (See Chapter Two.)

Protect Your Reputation

My ex and I owned a popular sports bar. Our target market was professionals over thirty. Therefore, our primary clientele consisted of married couples, singles and divorcees.

I have always been a people-watcher and over the years, I noticed that often, when people separate and divorce, they go a little crazy. It is probably very natural. However, be careful. Women almost always get judged. Men, not so much.

The women I observed were friends, acquaintances, and strangers. I saw some of them get a little too drunk and go home with different men. Maybe they didn't get **that** drunk or go home with **that** many men, but that was the perception.

I'm sure they were working through issues and were doing the best they could. I know I was. But unfortunately, perception is reality. And by the time these women were ready to have a real relationship, some of them had bad reputations.

I was making these observations while I was married, and because I was one of the bar's owners, I got an earful about some of them from the staff - as well as my spouse.

It bothered me because I knew some of these women. I knew why they were getting divorced. I knew what had happened to them, and I knew it wasn't their fault. Yet, because women are unfairly held to a different standard than men, the women were judged to be "loose" or "slutty".

So, when I started going through "The Big D" myself, I didn't want to get a bad reputation. I don't drink much to begin with, and I never went home with anyone from a bar. In fact, one night a male friend offered to give me a ride home. He and I have been friends for many years, and I am also friends with his wife. I decided to Uber instead. People talk where I'm from and sometimes they talk nonsense. I didn't want to take a chance on hurting anybody involved.

Maybe I was overly cautious and you won't need to be. Maybe where you live people don't love gossip. But in my experience, people love to talk about other people, especially when it makes them feel better about themselves. Ever notice that? People will tell the bad or untrue things more often than the good and up-lifting. Yes, it sucks.

Now, I'm not saying you have to live like a nun. I just want you to remember that this is temporary. Be careful what you do (or are perceived to do). It can come back to haunt you (and your kids).

Chapter 5

Find a Support Group

This really has nothing to do with the logistics of the divorce, but I think it is one of the most important thing I did.

I was in a 20-year relationship, 17 years of marriage, at the time of our separation. Over the course of that time, my ex convinced me I was stupid and worthless. He convinced me I couldn't survive without him. I honestly believe had his temper not turned violent that last night, and had it not happened while our son was home and could hear it, I would still be in that toxic marriage.

I didn't leave because I didn't think I could survive without him, and honestly, I didn't want to. I still loved him despite being terrified of him. I only left because I **couldn't** stay. I couldn't let our son experience anything like that night again. I was so scared for my safety, but all I could think about was the "what ifs" concerning our son.

What if he came downstairs and saw his dad acting like a madman? Would my ex turn on our child or would it snap him out of his rage? Or worse, what if our son didn't come downstairs but this time my ex made good on his threats? Would our son blame himself for not trying to save me? And finally, I didn't want my little boy (he was 12 years old at the time) to see his mom like that. I didn't want him to see me weak and terrified, locked in a tiny water closet, begging my husband, his father, not to hurt me.

A few months after we separated, a friend invited me to attend her 12-step recovery group. It is called Addiction Recovery Anonymous (ARA). It is a mixture of all kinds of addicts, as well as the family and friends of addicts. I went to that first meeting because I thought they would teach me how to "fix" my husband's alcohol problem and that would save my marriage. What I learned is I needed "fixin'" too. I learned I'm codependent. I needed to learn to detach and figure out who I was, with or without my husband.

I have learned a lot with the help of "my people". I've learned I'm actually smart. I'm actually really smart. I'm smarter than I thought I was, and I'm definitely smarter than he thought I was. (See Chapter Two)

I don't think I would have been strong enough to keep standing up for myself without the help of my group, and I really don't think I could have handled almost three years of divorce crap without their love and support. They have helped my self-esteem and that helps me be courageous and brave.

Find your people.

"Your people" don't necessarily have to be a 12-step program like mine is. Maybe you can find a divorce support group (I believe many churches have them). Is there something you used to enjoy doing that you don't do anymore? I have always loved dancing. My ex didn't dance. I started going dancing again with a girlfriend I met at the gym. Start doing whatever it is that used to make you happy and find other people to do it with. Make new friends. Find people who don't think of you as part of "Ken and Barbie". You are trying to make yourself whole again and to do that, you need people who will know and love Barbie. Just Barbie.

Be careful who you trust.

Divorce makes people crazy. People you have considered very close friends might turn their back on you. When my ex and I split, I had my best friend who lives almost 400 miles away, my mom, my sister and a couple of gym friends. ALL of my other "close" friends were the wives and girlfriends of his friends. Well, those people didn't stick around very long, and some of the things I confided in these women, got back to him.

I'm not saying this will happen to you. I'm simply advising you to be careful what you tell people. I didn't figure this out for the first year or two of my separation. It broke my heart, especially since some of them knew what was going on before I ever had the courage to admit it. Once I realized the duplicity of some people, I decided to assume everything I told people would get back to him.

Note: Once you figure out who these people are, you can tell them things you want him to know without directly telling him yourself. And even if it isn't true, he will believe it is because he heard it from someone you still "think" is your friend.

Chapter 6

Hire an Attorney Who Gives a Crap

Think about it...

If you end up going in front of a judge and jury, do you want someone who will just go through the motions? Or do you want someone who will REALLY try for you?

I don't think you necessarily need the "smartest" or the "best" attorney. Maybe the person you hire really is the best, but because he has only been practicing for five or six years, he doesn't have the reputation of being the best.

Also, you might not want the most combative attorney, but you don't want someone who will back down from a fight either.

I think finding the best attorney for **you** is more important than finding the "best" attorney.

My ex and I started out doing collaborative law. This is a fairly new way to get divorced. In case you don't know what this is, it is a less litigious way to get divorced. I describe it as a combination of sitting at the kitchen table splitting assets and mediation. Each party has an attorney and there are two neutral parties involved as well. The mental health expert keeps everyone on task. It's his job to keep people focused on splitting assets and not on the issues that led to the divorce. This neutral expert also helps with custody issues. You also have a neutral financial expert. This is the person who helps divide the money stuff. Both parties are supposed to provide their financial information and she helps the parties divide these assets.

I chose this type of divorce because I still loved my husband and I really didn't want a divorce, but I was afraid of him. I was afraid of him, and I didn't know if I would ever stop being afraid of him. At the time, I truly believed his alcohol problem and violent temper while inebriated were the problems. He promised to never lose his temper like that again, but he refused to stop drinking. I told him I was willing to try again if he would go to therapy for his anger issues, get back on his bipolar medication, and stop drinking.

He went to therapy. He absolutely refused to get back on his medication, and after almost three weeks of him trying to convince me he wasn't an alcoholic, he agreed to stop drinking. This lasted less than four weeks, and according to an extremely reliable source, "I don't think he ever quit."

The attorney I hired, Nevill Manning, has been my family's attorney for decades, and his daughter was my good friend growing up. He told me that if I want to have any chance of getting back together, we should do collaborative. He went on to say that if we ended up in court, we would end up hating each other. I couldn't stand the idea of the man I've loved half of my life hating me. So, I convinced my ex to do collaborative.

Now, I'm sure collaborative is great for some people. If both parties are willing to be transparent, I'm sure collaborative is a great option. However, my situation was different. I knew very little about our finances, and in seven months, my ex turned over three years of tax returns and a spreadsheet that he and one of his business partners concocted. I knew it was fictitious after looking at the very first line. FYI, anyone can make a spreadsheet. It doesn't mean it's factual in any way.

We had four collaborative sessions. My ex stormed out of three of them. His attorney was able to calm him down and convince him to come back twice. During our last collaborative meeting, when he didn't hear what he wanted, he stood up, turned to his attorney and said, "You're fired!" He then looked at me, and said, "We're going to court," and turned on his heel and stormed out.

Think of the kid on the playground taking his ball and going home if he doesn't get his way - this was my life.

So, after almost a year, he was forcing me to start all over. As an incentive for couples to not give up when the collaborative process gets tough, the parties must completely start over if they decide to quit collaborative and change to the traditional divorce process. Both parties have to hire new attorneys, and anyone involved in the collaborative process can't be involved going forward. As I'm sure you can imagine, this substantially increases the cost of divorce.

I didn't know what to do. I was terrified. I had already paid my attorney a small fortune, and now I was going to have to come up with money for another retainer??? All that time, energy, stress, heartache, and money got me nowhere. Nevill later told me we should not have gone the collaborative route because my ex was not committed to the process (aka - He was not willing to play fair) and starting over would cost me more money... money I didn't have.

Luckily, my attorney had known me since I was 15 years old. He recommended a couple of attorneys he thought could handle my case. He also told me to meet with a few others so my ex couldn't hire them. In Texas, any attorney one party pays to meet, can't even speak to the other party. Nevill wasn't sure these were the right attorneys for me, but these were great attorneys. And he didn't want my ex to have an opportunity to hire them.

Nevill recommended two attorneys and said both would have to be convinced to take my case because neither really does divorces anymore. He convinced the first one, Robin Green, to meet with me.

There was something I liked about Robin within minutes of meeting him. I told him the history of my marriage, what led up to the separation, and the collaborative experience. Robin agreed to take my case, but he wanted me to go home and think about it. He wanted me to be sure I was comfortable with him. He also told me to buy and read *Codependent No More* by Melody Beattie. I instantly knew this was my new attorney. I told him I had recently finished this book and her daily meditation book, *The Language of Letting Go* is what we use in my ARA meetings. This man cared about me and my situation. I never even met with the other guy. I know I flabbergasted him from time to time, but he always listened. I kept telling him that all I wanted was what is fair. He told me quite a few times that the law isn't fair and sometimes the bad guy wins. Well, I didn't like that. That's why I'm writing this book. Fairness matters. Doing the right thing matters. Honesty matters. And if it doesn't, it should. I want those things to matter again. I want good things to happen to good people and I want Karma to take care of the not-so-good people. Yes, I know I sound like a Pollyanna, but when did doing the right thing stop being the right thing to do?

Anyway, back to Robin. Sometimes he would tell me what I was focused on couldn't help my case, but sometimes what I couldn't stop focusing on led to the discovery of things that REALLY helped my case. In fact, at one point, Robin said to me, "There's your smoking gun."

So, find an attorney who listens to you and cares about you. If he can't remember the names of your kids, he doesn't care.

If he dismisses your ideas and concerns, he doesn't care. And if he constantly interrupts you or talks over you, he doesn't care. Let me say this again because it is very important - You NEED an attorney who cares.

After a few months working with Robin, a couple of issues came up concerning the safety and welfare of our son. Robin's specialty is financial law and although he practiced family law for many years, and even wrote a book about divorce, he didn't really do divorces anymore. He said he thought we needed to bring in someone who does a lot of family law. He thought we needed someone who was known (in a good way) by the family court judges. He vetted them and thought Ben Garcia was "our guy". Robin set a meeting so I could meet him and see if we clicked. Honestly, I wasn't sure about Ben at first. He is younger than I am (and I'm not that old yet). However, I really trusted Robin and if Robin thought Ben was the right guy for my case, I was going to hire him. This is another way I believe my higher power was leading me. Ben became invaluable to me. At first, I wasn't sure if he cared. My feelings and needs had been ignored for so long that I needed my fears, beliefs, and ideas to be validated. I NEEDED to be heard. He did that. Ben not only heard me, he told me I was right... most of the time. He has even told me at least half a dozen times that I should go to law school. He says I'm really good at this. We'll see.

So, Robin was my lead attorney and Ben was there to help with custody stuff. Then a little thing called COVID-19 happened. After eight months of trying to get a temporary orders hearing, the pre-trial date was set-DURING THE FREAKIN' SHUTDOWN. We had to meet with the judge via Zoom. He told us to work out temporary orders ourselves and if we couldn't, we would have a hearing. That was in April. I tried to get temporary orders agreed upon without the judge, but the other side either ignored or, after weeks of waiting for a response, refused my offers. They never once sent a counteroffer about temporary orders.

Finally, after a year of trying to get a temporary orders hearing, my ex decided he wanted to kick me and our son out of our home. After a year of his attorneys not being "available" on the same day for a hearing, they suddenly were when my ex was the one who wanted the hearing. Due to COVID-19 and Robin's age, he couldn't go to court that day. When I finally got to go in front of the judge it had been 994 days going through this mess. It had been 994 days since I finally stood up to the man I loved and said, "NO MORE!" And honestly, 994 days still a little brainwashed by him. It was 994 days of him telling me no one would believe me. Well, it took 994 days and even though he sold his lies to quite a few people, the one person that mattered in the eyes of the law saw right through him. The one person who mattered saw the actual evidence and listened to the testimonies and made his decision. He heard one person lie under oath and he saw the evidence in black and white to prove he was lying. I was prepared for his lies. I knew he would try to convince the judge using his version of the truth. And believe it or not, even though I had proof, until the judge made his ruling, part of me was terrified that this would be one more person who would fall for his fiction. It took 994 days, but I was finally vindicated. The truth came out (only pertaining to child welfare and financial issues) and the honest side won that battle. I did my homework and gave it to Ben. We were ready. We were prepared. And almost every time my ex made an untrue statement, I flipped through my binders and pulled out the truth. And Ben was amazing. My point is it is really important to do your homework. Go through every piece of discovery yourself. But it doesn't matter how prepared you are if your attorney won't hear you. If he won't use the knowledge and facts you provide, it doesn't matter how good he is.

So, I'm going to say it a third time — HIRE AN ATTORNEY WHO CARES.

Side note: I kind of miss my attorneys. I feel bonded to them. They helped me put my life back together. Not only did they fight for me, but they also fought for my son. They saw me when I needed to be seen. They heard me when I needed to be heard. Find attorneys like that.

Chapter 7

Get Your Divorce "Degree"

Talk to people who have experienced this and won.

How did they do it? What worked? What didn't work.

You wouldn't ask someone who has never jumped out of a plane to teach you to skydive. You will be surprised how often people want to help others going through similar experiences (this book for example).

Similarly, talk to people who have experienced this and lost.

What do they wish they had done differently? How did their actions affect their children?

Failure is the greatest teacher. Let their failures teach you. Good people do good things. And there are still good people in the world. Let these people help you.

Oh, and don't limit these conversations only to women. Ask men too. Get that perspective.

Educate Yourself

Learn everything you can. The NBC public service announcement series "The More You Know" says it perfectly. Not only will you learn about your case and what to expect, you will also become an invaluable tool to help your attorneys.

And the greatest part of this for me?

Empowerment.

I felt like I had no control over my own life or the welfare of our child.

He had control of our money.

He had control of our businesses.

When we got our taxes each year, he told me where to sign and I did. I didn't know anything.

So here I was knowing nothing. I had to ask my ex questions about our finances and businesses. The hardest part was trying to discern what was fact and what was fiction. I can tell you there was a whole lot of fiction, but the more I felt something wasn't right, the more I questioned. The more I questioned, the more I questioned my attorneys. The more they looked, the more they found. The more we found, the more questions we had. We just uncovered more and more.

For twenty years I believed every word out of his mouth. And, for twenty years, he knew I believed every word out of his mouth. I don't think he expected me to question him. Why would he? I never had. Maybe this was his fatal flaw (see Chapter Two). This is how I really found out things were amiss. I asked him questions. But I didn't stop there. I asked trusted and knowledgeable friends if his answers sounded right. I asked about things that didn't make sense to me AND I asked about things that made perfect sense to me. I knew I had been controlled and brainwashed for twenty years. When I still didn't trust my gut, I asked others for guidance. This not only helped my case, but it also helped my self-confidence. I was learning to trust myself when something didn't make sense. I wasn't "stupid" or "worthless" after all. Who woulda guessed?

Honestly, I feel like I did this. It wasn't just my attorneys (although they definitely did the heavy lifting). I brought down Goliath. Everything was stacked against me. So, I educated myself. I went through everything. You can too. Empower yourself! You are amazing. You just don't know it yet.

Chapter 8

Look Through Every Piece of Discovery Yourself

And when you finish, do it again.

When I started this journey, I thought my attorney would go through all of the discovery. The truth is, they don't have time to go through all of it and most attorneys don't have enough staff to do it for them. And, if you are like me, you can't afford the billable hours it would take them to go through it all. It's not like it is on television with all of these people looking through thousands of pages of discovery to find the smoking gun. You have to be your own *Erin Brockovich.* You can find your own smoking gun.

I went through all of it because I was on a budget. I thought anything I could do myself, would save money. I didn't have access to our community funds and now I'm grateful for that. I might have assumed they were doing it, and there were things I found that I'm not sure anyone else would have found. You might see something that looks out of place but may not draw your attorney's attention.

Go through bank and credit card statements and cross reference them with your calendar, text messages, and social media. You have no idea what you might find. Also, if you own businesses, go to your state's Secretary of State website. Find the documents. Look at the dates on each document to find changes.

Remember - You may feel like you don't know your husband at all anymore, but you do. You probably know him better than anyone else in the world. And, if something doesn't look right, it probably isn't.

Preparation is key!

If you are going on a trip, you prepare. You check the weather so you can pack the appropriate clothing. If you are driving, you make sure your oil has been changed, your tires have been rotated, and you have plenty of gas. I'm a list-maker. I have a packing checklist in the notes of my phone. Don't want to forget my phone charger.

Likewise, prepare for your divorce. Not only will you feel better, you will do better. And you will be more confident.

I am a huge sports fan. Have you ever noticed that the team who is better prepared usually wins? They practice. They anticipate situations. You need to anticipate situations.

Are y'all fighting over the house? Anticipate his argument and then derail it.

Is he going to call you an unfit mother? Prepare your rebuttal. Has he given you Mother's Day cards that say you are the best mom he could have ever asked for? Maybe you have text conversations or social media posts that prove this is untrue.

Whatever it is, there are only two people that actually know the truth. The person who is most prepared will convince the judge or jury.

Chapter 9

Read EVERYTHING - And Ask Questions

Unless you have a law degree, you won't understand everything. Ask questions. It doesn't make you a dumb blonde. It makes you someone who doesn't have a law degree. It makes you someone who is going through something terrifying that you have never experienced before. I think it is imperative to ask questions. This will affect the rest of your life. Don't you want to know and understand everything?

Also, nobody is perfect. Everyone makes mistakes... Possibly even a badass attorney who cares about you.

Read every single word of every single document, and if you don't understand something, ask questions. I know it is overwhelming. Only the legal system needs three pages to say what you and I say in a few sentences. And if you are like me, you don't know what this legal mumbo jumbo means. Read it anyway. With your own eyes. And ask questions. This is your life we are talking about. This is your children's lives we are talking about. Your attorney might accidentally miss something. He (or she) is human. If you don't read everything and ask questions, it could cost you. I very seriously doubt the other side will bring it to your attention. They aren't going to say, "Oh yeah, we know what you meant. That's okay."

It's up to you, Blondie. Read EVERYTHING. QUESTION and ask for clarification on anything and everything you don't understand.

Chapter 10

Don't Forget Your WHY

Don't forget why you are ending your marriage. It might be the same reason you stayed.

I stayed because I was in an abusive marriage. I was being controlled and manipulated and I didn't think I was capable of living without him. He was gaslighting me to the point I truly thought I had early onset dementia. That is why I started saving our texts years before we separated and why I recorded some of our conversations in the beginning. I wasn't trying to be this master super sleuth legal person, and I had no idea these conversations would end up helping me. I was actually afraid I was losing my mind!

The mental and emotional abuse was so bad that he had me convinced it was MY fault he lost his temper. He actually told me I MADE him treat me that way. According to him, I made him punch holes in our walls and doors; I guess I also made him terrify me to the point of locking myself in the bathroom. The problem was, I freakin' believed him. He was so great sometimes. So, when he wasn't, it must have been my fault. I tried and tried to be better. Imagine the mouse running on the wheel. If it doesn't get cheese sometimes, it will quit running. I was the mouse.

In the beginning, I stayed (and went back to him) because I not only loved him, I loved his daughter. I fell for that girl the moment I met her, and she even called me her "sucker" when she was a little girl. So, I let him get away with things I never would have let any other guy get away with because I didn't want to lose either one of them. I was playing house and it felt great. But I loved her and I lost her anyway.

Another reason I stayed was because I didn't want to break up our family. My parents divorced when I was 15 years old, and I felt pulled between the two sides. I didn't want that for our son. I never wanted to be divorced.

Eventually, I left for our son. I had to stop the cycle. Men learn how to treat women based on how they see their mothers treated. I refuse to let our son fall in love someday and constantly break her heart because he thinks the way his father treated me is the way he should treat a woman. I let him see it for the first 12 years of his life. I hope, pray, and have to believe it's not too late.

Stay True to Yourself

Just because you think, or know, he is doing something shady, doesn't mean you should too. I believe if you take the emotions out of things (very hard for me by the way), most things in life are pretty black-and-white. There are very few shades of grey.

If you say to yourself, "I know I'm not supposed to do this, but I know he is." Don't do it, Blondie. If you say, "I know I shouldn't talk about this to our kids, but I know he is, and I just want them to have my side of the story too." Go to the first part of the sentence, to the word "but". Delete the rest.

I know this is really hard, and I know how hard it is to do this knowing the rest of the world is believing the lies told about you. But for me, I need to be able to look myself in the mirror and know I'm a good person. I need to be able to look in our son's eyes and feel confident that I am a good mother.

Now don't get me wrong, I've had my fair share of screw-ups (I still do from time to time). Learn from my mistakes. I'm learning from them. Just don't change your core values and who you are to win. I believe that if you do, in the end, you will lose the most. You will lose yourself.

Don't beat yourself up if (when) you slip.

You are mourning. This is a huge loss.

I'm still mourning. I'm not mourning the loss of my husband anymore. I'm mourning the loss of the man I thought he would be once he realized how much I loved him and how much he was hurting me (yes, I now know that was very co-dependent thinking). And I'm mourning the loss of the "happily ever after" he promised me.

I'm also mourning the loss of my family. I am losing half of the time that is left with our son before he goes to college. The once special relationship I had with my bonus baby (I always liked that term better than stepdaughter) is now nonexistent. I hope we can find our way back to each other, and I'll never stop hoping, but I can't force the relationship. We can't make people love us, and sometimes trying too hard pushes them further away. But I will never stop loving her and missing her.

The grief is real and can be overwhelming, even if you are the one who ultimately asked for the divorce.

So, if you don't ALWAYS do everything right, it's okay. Give yourself a break.

Oh, and it's okay to be angry. I am still a little angry (and some days I'm more angry than others). I'm angry that I lost my happily ever after. I'm angry that I am losing this time with my son. I am angry that I have lost the relationship with my bonus baby. I'm angry my husband refused to be a better man. I'm angry that I stayed true to myself and what I felt to be the right thing to do, yet people chose him... People chose him who admitted they "know you can only believe half of what he says." One person even said, "and for the record, I don't believe anything he has said about you since the separation." Manipulators manipulate. That's what they do. And like attracts like. The liars and character deficient will choose the person with like characteristics. And I'm angry that I lost all of these things when HE was the abuser; HE was the liar and schemer. But most of all, I'm still angry at myself for not speaking up for myself sooner. I deserved better but I believed him when he told me, "No one else will ever love you." I believed him when he told me I made him lose his temper. And I'm angry at myself for spending so much time walking on eggshells and trying to keep him happy so he wouldn't take his love away from me.

So, feel the anger. Work through it. And then, let it go. That's what I'm trying to do. In the meantime, give yourself a little grace. We deserve it.

Chapter 11

Know When to Walk Away - Know When to RUN

The law of diminishing returns is used to refer to the point at which the level of profits or benefits gained is less than the amount of money or energy invested.

I truly believe that if I had refused to settle, I would have ended up with a lot more financially. I found a few shady things that would have cost him had we gone to court.

I believe the judge would have split our community estate in a way that would have given me at least 65% due to the factors the courts in the state of Texas use to determine a "fair and just" division of property. I also believe the jury would have awarded me damages for the domestic abuse. Once the temporary orders transcript proving he lied to the judge multiple times was introduced, they wouldn't believe anything he said. Even if they did, I had proof of the abuse.

Also, in Texas anyway, everything is considered community property unless the party claiming it is separate property proves with "clear and convincing evidence" it is separate. I don't believe my ex would have been able to meet this burden.

However, from day one, I said I wouldn't go after the business entities that actually belonged to his father (but were on our taxes). I believed this was his separate property regardless of what was "provable". (See Chapter Ten.)

All I wanted is what was fair. My half. It was already my money. I just had no access to it.

So even though I am almost certain I would have walked away with a lot more, possibly double, I had to stay true to my values. And once he agreed to "give" me what I believed was half, I decided it was time to walk away.

My divorce proceedings lasted almost three years. My ex stalled and his attorneys played the legal system to avoid court. When he decided he needed it to end, his attorneys' schedules miraculously opened up. After the temporary orders hearing, he saw the writing on the wall (or his attorneys spelled it out for him). He was now willing to make a deal to keep it out of court. I could have forced a jury hearing. Part of me really wanted the world to know what he had done to me. I wanted the people I once considered friends to know what he is like so they would feel bad for taking his side. But I realized that's not what really mattered to me. I could have done it, but at what cost? Would it really be worth it?

My 'Why' is our son. He needed this to end. I needed this to end, too. We needed to start the next chapter of our lives (pun intended). We needed to heal and grow.

How far should you take it? Only you can answer that question.

Chapter 12

Take Care of Yourself

Don't let your divorce take over your life. The "what ifs" and the "I've gotta do thats" will make you crazy if you let them. There for a while, all I did was worry about my divorce. I couldn't eat; I couldn't sleep. All I did was worry about the future I would have with our son when this was all over. I lost a lot of weight but not in a good way. I looked sickly. I think my skin aged 10 years in the first year because of the stress, fear, and malnutrition. And... my dirty-blonde hair (pre highlights) that had just a tad bit of gray by my ears, now has so much gray that Danny, my amazing hairdresser, friend, and cheerleader, has probably seen more of me in the last three years than in the ten previous ones.

What I'm trying to say in my own quirky way is this:

Don't let the stress and anxiety suck all of the joy (or your hair color) out of your life. I should have included money in the settlement for the extra botox and hair color my ex cost me. Lol

Try to do one thing each day that makes you happy. Do one thing that makes you smile. Between the divorce, kids, work, and whatever other stressors you have in your life, you might think you don't have any time left for yourself. Do one thing that makes you happy. Maybe you love Chick-fil-A. It only takes a few minutes to stop and get yourself your favorite meal. You can take a short walk or go to the gym. You could meditate or pray or call your best friend.

I was not only going through a divorce, I was trying to figure out who I was. As an abused woman, I became someone else. I became someone I couldn't look at in the mirror. I hated who I had become, and I didn't know how much of this version of me was actually me or who he groomed me to be. So, I started trying new things. I tried painting. I'm not great but there is something about the brush strokes that is very calming. Next, I started crafting a little. I make wreaths for any occasion and have had two people actually offer to pay for them. Many people have told me I should make them and sell them on Etsy. Maybe I will.

After the divorce, I sold the house and downsized. At the time, the housing market was crazy, and houses were selling in a matter of days (even hours). I bought a house that I really liked - but didn't love. I designed my own accent wall and I love love love it. This Christmas, I made two garlands. The first one turned out pretty great, and I was really proud of my accomplishment. So, I made one for my mantle too.

My most recent "New Thing" is learning to sew. I told my mom I was thinking of learning, and she surprised me with a sewing machine. When I was a child, my mom made all of her clothes, as well as the clothes for me and my sister. She is an incredible seamstress and even made heavy black theater curtains for my last house. She really can make just about anything. I made two faux fur body pillowcases. And I'm going to toot my own horn for a minute, they aren't bad. Next, I need to learn how to sew the zippers into them.

My point is that you can try something new. Heck, I even wrote this book!!!

Chapter 13

Every Little Bit Helps

Even the smallest detail matters.

So here you are. You want to help yourself. You want to be brave and prove to the world you aren't just some stupid woman. You want to prove to HIM you aren't some stupid woman. You want to prove to yourself you aren't stupid. And, if you are like me, you want your children to respect you.

Giant leaps? No. Baby steps. Think about a child's first steps. They are scared but determined. I was scared but determined. I'm sure you are scared. Let that fear feed your determination. I was terrified that my ex would make good on his threats to leave me penniless. I knew I had to do everything I could to keep him from manipulating the system. You can too!

"Make small decisions with the big picture in mind."

It makes perfect sense to me now. I didn't end up in a bad marriage overnight. It wasn't one decision either of us made or didn't make. It wasn't one thing one of us did or didn't do. And it wasn't one thing we said or didn't say. It was a million little things. Sometimes, I would let something slide because I didn't want to argue. Then, the next time it happened, he would say, "Why is this a problem now when it wasn't before?" I also said yes to some little things I didn't want to do to make him happy. Those little things evolved into bigger and bigger things. They snowballed to the point that when I looked in the mirror, I didn't know who I was anymore. I really struggled to figure out how I got to that point. And, I hated the person I had become. I turned myself into the woman he wanted me to be, and I didn't like her very much.

What I have learned is that this didn't happen overnight, and I can't fix it overnight.

Here are a few of my favorite sayings from Al-Anon and AA:
"It's about progress, not perfection."
"Take one day at a time."
"Just do the next right thing."

Make a small decision. When I first separated from my ex, I couldn't make even the smallest decision for myself. I remember a friend asking me where I would like to eat. I *really* couldn't decide. Eventually, I was able to decide where to eat. Once you start making small decisions, it becomes easier to make medium-sized decisions, and then you can make larger decisions.

Do you think a girl who couldn't decide on a restaurant would ever consider writing a book when this started? Yet here I am.

And, sometimes, I didn't make decisions because I was afraid. I was afraid of making the wrong decision, so I didn't make any decision at all. I've learned that not making a decision IS a decision. The more decisions you make, the better you will get at it. It's like everything else in this life - it takes practice.

Don't let this hold you back. "So, take the risks. Make the big moves, even if they're small moves. Forge ahead with your lives in any and every direction that moves you," Rebecca

Pearson, *This is Us*. I love this quote because I am trying to live this way. I have spent most of my life paralyzed by fear. I feared being myself because others might not like, let alone love, me. I feared standing up for myself and what I wanted (or didn't want) with my ex because I feared he would leave me, for good this time.

I know you are scared. I was too. Honestly, sometimes I still am. But you have a choice. Decide right now, today, that you will get through this. Decide you will be happy. We believe what we tell ourselves more than we believe what others tell us. Tell yourself you are strong. Tell yourself you are capable. Tell yourself you are smart. And tell yourself you are beautiful and kind and WORTHY. Tell yourself all of these things and anything else you need to hear. Then, keep telling yourself. Eventually, you will believe them.

And remember, this is just a phase. However, this is a phase that will have a lasting effect on the rest of your life. So put in the work. If you want (or need) your life to change, you have to change it. Accept help from others but you need to know 100% without a doubt that YOU can do this. Trust me, if I can, anybody can.

I believe in you, Blondie.

Chapter 14

Dumb Blonde?

It took me 35 months to get divorced. I believe my ex was dragging things out in hopes I would run out of money to pay my attorneys. I would then have to accept whatever he was willing to give me. Trust me, his offers were not only small, they were laughable and a slap in the face considering we were married for 20 years, I am the mother of his son, and I loved his daughter as my own for 23 years. But why would he start playing fair in our divorce when he didn't play fair in our marriage? Why would he treat me with respect now when he hadn't before? Regardless, his "game plan" is just my opinion.

These are the provable facts:

1. He perjured himself multiple times on the stand during our first hearing. After trying to get a temporary orders hearing for over a year, and his attorneys being "unavailable" for each date, he decided he wanted to kick me and our son out of our home. He wanted the judge to make us move out so he could sell the house. He claimed that the house only had a sixth of the equity it had, and since his father loaned us the money, we didn't own it. Remember

how I told you to never delete text messages? Well, I had a text message from my ex that stated his dad was forgiving part of the loan each year for accounting work my ex was doing for him. Boom—the house just became paid for and since it was paid for by income (accounting work), it was community property.
2. We caught him committing fraud-more than once. First, one of my amazing attorneys looked at a document that I kept asking about because something "felt off" about it. Well, I was right. He signed one of our assets over to his father. Maybe he thought nobody would notice since they have the same name.
3. The second time we caught him committing fraud is when his father passed away. Now, I think this is really what got the settlement going because it probably would have landed at least one of his attorneys in hot water with the state bar association. One day, I was looking at his father's will. I was looking at it because he mentioned it in the hearing. It had been filed so one of my attorneys pulled it to look over. As I was looking at it, I noticed the date it was signed, and my ex had signed as a witness... in Florida. I didn't think my ex had been in Florida at that time. So, what did I do? I went to the text messages. And guess what? He was at a Texas Tech baseball game that day. I wasn't at that game because that is the same day we got our new puppy. We texted about the puppy and the game. He even texted to say he was stopping for a beer at our bar. And, nope, our bar is not in Florida. So, then I looked at the notary. The notary was a guy who worked for my ex and his father for many years, and I considered a friend. His notary stamp said it expired in four years and 76 days after the will was supposedly signed. Some good friends of mine came over one day and one of them googled "notary state of Texas". Turns

out, a notary stamp is only good for four years. Seventy-six days. Seventy-six days gave me "clear and convincing evidence" beyond the text messages that my father-in-law's will was not signed when it was dated. Something else fishy is that the will said it was created in Florida, but it was notarized by a Texas notary. My attorney sent letters to the notary asking for the signature pages of his notary book. By law, a notary is required to turn over any pages requested by any citizen. He never sent the pages. One day, my attorneys and I were on a zoom meeting (Covid). I was talking about all of these discrepancies. Robin stopped me and said, "The will is invalid." He said, "In the state of Texas, a named person in a will can't be a witness to said will." My ex was named executor of the will and was a witness.

Those are the facts. My opinion is that once we requested the notary ledger, everyone freaked out. This wasn't just about screwing me out of my half anymore. This was now about making sure the will wasn't invalidated. You see, my father-in-law was a wealthy man, and he left my ex in control of everything. In fact, my ex holds the purse strings of every member of his family. If that will had been invalidated, and the fraud (and conspiracy to commit fraud) was revealed, he would have lost that control. So, he quit fighting over our relatively small assets to ensure he kept control of his father's estate. I also believe the attorney who filed this invalid will was afraid of disbarment.

Again, this is only my opinion, but if you have learned anything, I am NOT a dumb blonde. And that, my friend, is how I took my power back. That is how I learned to fight for what's right for myself.

Take your power back! Fight for yourself! Fight for what's fair! You can do it! I know you can! You are not a dumb blonde! You are a BLONDIE!!!

Robin Green (1944-2021)
You told me to write a book. I wrote it.
I wish you could have read it.

Acknowledgements

To the God of my understanding - Thank you for bringing these people, and others, into my life when You knew I would need them. Thank you for giving me the gifts to help others in similar situations to mine. And thank you for loving me when I didn't think You did, and I didn't think You should.

Amy - Thank you for being my best friend, my biggest cheerleader, my shoulder to cry on, and my rock. Thank you for always loving me even when I thought you wouldn't. You will never know how precious the gift of your friendship is to me.

Chris - Thank you for calling me every day so I knew I wasn't alone. Thank you for calming my fears when I was terrified. And thank you for reminding me I am Jennipop! **And Jill**, thank you for sending him to do my "man chores," for supporting me, and for letting us have our friendship.

Carl - Your giant hugs are as healing as your words. Thank you for being a friend, a confidant, a guide, a guru, an editor, and the "grandfather figure" you thought I needed. As usual, you were right.

Dr. Judith Wilkins - Judy, thank you for being my safe space to admit what was going on in my marriage. You were the first person I told, and I was terrified. You helped me find my strength, strength I now believe I've always possessed. Thank you for holding my hand through the process. You told me more than once that every decision I make, or don't make, is based on fear and you were right. I'm still afraid but I'm making progress.

Lisa - Thank you for making me leave my house and for making me eat.

Danny - Thank you for being part hairdresser, part therapist, and all friend.

To the members of ARA - One of the best days of my life is the day I walked into that room. I love each of you. You were here for me when I was at my lowest. Thank you for cheering on my progress, supporting my setbacks, and drying my tears when I couldn't hold myself together anymore. I now know I don't always have to hold myself together. I am grateful for all I have learned from each of you.

To my attorneys (in the order hired)-
Nevill - You said you don't fail very often. We did not get this done together but you did not fail me. Everything happened as it was meant to happen. I will always be grateful for your help.
Robin - Thank you for taking my case. Thank you for believing in me. Thank you for holding my hand and listening to me as much as I thank you for your legal genius. And thank you for gifting it all to me. Nobody has ever touched my heart like that.
Ben - Thank you for listening to my fears and worst-case-scenarios. Thank you for telling me more times than I can count to go to law school. You helped me believe I'm

smart...not just some dumb blonde. And thank you for kicking butt in court.

Heather - You are my sister by the Grace of God, and I am eternally grateful.

Mom - One of the best things about my divorce is the opportunity it gave me to reconnect with you. I love you.

Ed - Thank you for having my back, Pops. And thank you for loving my mom the way she always deserved to be loved.

Blake - Thank you for teaching me about the unconditional love of and for a child. From the beginning, you stole my heart, and I knew I would love no matter what, for the rest of my life. In my heart, you will always be my Honey Bun, my bonus baby.

And finally, Brooks - Thank you for being My Sunshine. You make it all worth it. You are the greatest love of my life. My Greatest Blessing. My cup runneth over.

Jenni Avery is the first-time author of *The Dumb Blonde's Guide to Divorce*. However, she is not dumb, and she is now only chemically blonde. After graduating from Texas Tech University with a bachelor's degree in Public Relations, she worked in Media Relations for the minor league baseball teams in Indianapolis and Las Vegas. She dreamed of working for the Chicago Cubs but came back to Lubbock after falling in love with her future husband/ex-husband and his daughter from his first marriage. She worked as a make-up artist for years before she and her then husband opened their own Planet Beach franchise and had their son. Jenni has always loved building people up and helping their self-esteem, first with makeup, then with her tanning spa, and now with *The Dumb Blonde's Guide to Divorce*. Her writing is concise, easy to follow, and meant to help readers navigate divorce as a friend would help them.

After her divorce, she sold her spa and is working as a makeup artist in addition to helping others with her experience, strength, and love.

Originally from Whitharral, Texas and currently living in Lubbock, she spends her free time with her son, his cat, and their two Frenchies, Theo and Ivy. She also loves travelling and attending concerts. Matchbox 20 is her all-time favorite band. And, during baseball season, she can almost always be found watching her beloved Cubs.

Learn more at **thedumbblondesguide.com**

CPSIA information can be obtained
at www.ICGtesting.com
Printed in the USA
BVHW050052250223
659171BV00011B/1464

9 781957 864693